**Bush
Theatre**

GUARDS
AT
THE
TAJ

by Rajiv Joseph

7 April – 20 May 2017
Bush Theatre, London

Developed at the Lark Play Development Center, New York City.
World premiere presented by Atlantic Theater Company,
New York City, 2015.

Cast

Humayun	**Danny Ashok**
Babur	**Darren Kuppan**

Creative Team

Playwright	**Rajiv Joseph**
Director	**Jamie Lloyd**
Designer	**Soutra Gilmour**
Lighting Designer	**Richard Howell**
Sound Design & Composition	**George Dennis**
Fight Director	**Kate Waters**
Costume Supervisor	**Lydia Crimp**
Company Stage Manager	**Vicky Eames**
Assistant Stage Manager	**Remi Bruno Smith**
Set Builder	**TIN SHED Scenery**
Associate Producers	**Homer Simpson Productions**

The Bush would like to thank Roger Wingate of Act Productions, White Light, Tom Gladstone and the team at Lyric Hammersmith and James Lewis at Tin Shed Scenery.

The Associate Producers wish to thank Stage One and Mayank Patel for their support.

Cast

Danny Ashok Humayun

Danny's theatre credits include *Disgraced* (Lyceum Theatre, Broadway), *The Djinns of Eidgah* (Royal Court Theatre), *Disgraced* (Bush Theatre), *The Royal Duchess Superstore* (The Barking Broadway), *Henry IV Parts 1 & 2* (Theatre Royal Bath) and *Blood & Gifts* (National Theatre).

Television includes *Capital*, *The Five*, *Holby City*, *The Dumping Ground*, *Casualty*, *Coronation Street* and *The Bill*. Films include: *Finding Fatimah*, *Four Lions*, *Perfume*, *The Wasp* and *The Caterpillar*.

Darren Kuppan Babur

Darren's theatre credits include *Cymbeline* (Shakespeare's Globe Theatre), *The Tempest* (Shakespeare's Globe Theatre), *Cast The Light* (Walk The Plank), *East Is East* (Trafalgar Studios & Tour), *An August Bank Holiday Lark* (Northern Broadsides), *Melody Loses Her Mojo* (20 Stories High), *England Street* (Oxford Playhouse), *Much Ado About Nothing* (RSC), *We Love You City* (Belgrade/Talking Birds), *Great Expectations* (ETT/Watford Palace), *Christmas Carol* (Library Theatre), *Rafta Rafta* (Bolton Octagon/New Vic Stoke), *Aladdin* (Theatre Royal Stratford East), *Jamaica House* (The Dukes Playhouses), *Arabian Nights* (New Vic Stoke) and *Bollywood Jane* (West Yorkshire Playhouse).

Television includes *Coronation Street*, *Spooks*, *Britannia High*, *Emmerdale* and *The Adam & Shelley Show*.

Creative Team

Rajiv Joseph Playwright

Rajiv Joseph's Broadway play *Bengal Tiger at the Baghdad Zoo* was a 2010 Pulitzer Prize finalist for drama, and also awarded a grant for Outstanding New American Play by the National Endowment for the Arts. Joseph's New York productions include *Guards at the Taj* (Atlantic Theater Company, 2015) which was awarded the 2016 Obie award for Best New Play and the Lucille Lortel award for Outstanding Play, *The North Pool* (Vineyard Theater, 2013), *Gruesome Playground Injuries* (Second Stage Theatre, 2011), *Animals Out of Paper* (Second Stage Theatre, 2008), *The Leopard and the Fox* (Alter Ego, 2007), *Huck & Holden* (Cherry Lane Theatre, 2006), and *All This Intimacy* (Second Stage Theatre, 2006). Other recent plays include *Mr. Wolf* (South Coast Repertory, 2015), *The Lake Effect* (Crossroads Theatre in New Jersey, 2013) and *Monster at the Door* (Alley Theatre in Houston, 2011).

Rajiv wrote for the Showtime series *Nurse Jackie* for seasons 3 and 4 and was the co-screenwriter of the film *Draft Day*, starring Kevin Costner and Jennifer Garner. He is the book-writer and co-lyricist for the musical, *Fly*, which premiered at the Dallas Theater Center in 2013. Jack Perla and Rajiv's opera *Shalimar the Clown*, adapted from the novel by Salman Rushdie, recently had its highly anticipated world premiere at the Opera Theatre of Saint Louis. The Wall Street Journal called Joseph's libretto "a remarkably succinct and faithful distillation" of Rushdie's novel.

He received his BA in Creative Writing from Miami University and his MFA in Dramatic Writing from NYU's Tisch School of the Arts. He served for three years in the Peace Corps in Senegal and now lives in Brooklyn.

Jamie Lloyd Director

Jamie's recent work, presented by The Jamie Lloyd Company, includes *The Maids*, *The Homecoming*, *The Ruling Class*, *Richard III*, *The Pride*, *The Hothouse* and the Olivier Award-nominated *Macbeth* (all at Trafalgar Studios). His other work includes *The Pitchfork Disney*, *Killer* (Shoreditch Town Hall), *Assassins* (Menier Chocolate Factory; Evening Standard Award nomination for Best Director), *Urinetown* (St James & Apollo), *The Commitments*

(Palace), *Cyrano de Bergerac* (Roundabout Theatre Company; American Airlines Theatre, Broadway), *The Duchess of Malfi* (Old Vic), *She Stoops to Conquer* (National Theatre; WhatsOnStage Award nomination for Best Revival), *The Faith Machine*, the Olivier Award-winning *The Pride* (Royal Court), *Inadmissible Evidence*, *The 25th Annual Putnam County Spelling Bee*, the Evening Standard Award-winning *Passion*, *Polar Bears* (Donmar Warehouse) and *Piaf* (Donmar Warehouse, Vaudeville Theatre, Teatro Liceo in Buenos Aires and Nuevo Teatro Alcala in Madrid; Olivier Award nomination for Best Musical Revival, Hugo Award for Best Director, Clarin Award for Best Musical Production, ADEET Award for Best Production).

For radio, he directed and co-adapted *Orson Welles' Heart of Darkness* (BBC Radio 4). He was Associate Director of the Donmar Warehouse from 2008 to 2011, a former Associate Artist of Headlong and the Macgeorge Fellow with the University of Melbourne in 2016.

Soutra Gilmour Designer

Soutra's theatre credits include *Strictly Ballroom, Les Blancs, Evening at the Talk House* (costume), *Light Shining in Buckinghamshire* (costume), *Strange Interlude, Antigone* (Evening Standard Award, Best Design), *Moon on a Rainbow Shawl, Double Feature, Shadow of a Boy* (all National Theatre), *Hecuba, Candide, The Tragedy of Thomas Hobbes* (RSC), *The Commitments* (Palace Theatre) *From Here to Eternity* (Shaftesbury), *Urinetown* (Apollo/St James Theatre), *Dr Faustus, The Homecoming, The Ruling Class, Richard III, The Pride, The Hothouse, Macbeth* (Jamie Lloyd Company/Trafalgar Transformed), *Merrily We Roll Along* (Menier Chocolate Factory/Harold Pinter), *Assassins, Torchsong Trilogy* (Menier Chocolate Factory), *Cyrano de Bergerac* (Roundabout, New York; Tony nomination Best Costume Design), *The Duchess of Malfi* (Old Vic), *Reasons to be Pretty* (Almeida), *Inadmissible Evidence* (Evening Standard Award, Best Design), *Piaf* (Donmar Warehouse, Vaudeville Theatre, Teatro Liceo in Buenos Aires and Nuevo Teatro Alcala in Madrid; Olivier nomination for Best Revival), *Polar Bears* (Donmar), *In a Forest Dark and Deep* (Vaudeville), *Reasons to be Happy* (Hampstead Theatre) *The Little Dog Laughed* (Garrick), *Three Days of Rain* (Apollo), *Who's Afraid of Virginia Woolf, Close the Coalhouse Door, Our Friends in the North, Ruby Moon* and *Son of Man* (Northern Stage), *The Pride* (Olivier nomination, Outstanding Achievement), *The Lover/The Caretaker* (Olivier nomination, Best Set Design), *The Collection* (Comedy), *Angels in America* (Lyric, Hammersmith), *Baby Doll, Thérèse Raquin* (Citizens Theatre), *Bad Jazz, A Brief History of Helen of Troy* (ATC; TMA nomination, Best Touring Production), *The Birthday Party, The Caretaker* (Sheffield Crucible/Tricycle), *Bull* (Sheffield Crucible/ Brits on Broadway, Young Vic), *Hair* (WhatsOnStage; Time Out Live nominations), *Witness* (Gate Theatre) and *Ghost City* (Arcola, New York).

Richard Howell Lighting Designer

Richard's credits include *Jekyll and Hyde* (Old Vic), *The Homecoming, East is East* (Trafalgar Studios), *Privacy* (Donmar Warehouse and Public Theater, New York), *Bad Jews* (Theatre Royal Bath, West End and UK Tour), *Labyrinth* (Hampstead Theatre), *Plastic, 4000 Miles,* (Ustinov, Bath), *The Wild Party* (The Other Palace), *Breaking The Code, A Doll's House, Little Shop of Horrors* (Manchester Royal Exchange), *The Glass Menagerie* (Headlong, UK Tour), *I See You* (Royal Court), *Playing For Time* (Sheffield Crucible), *The Grinning Man, The Crucible* and *The Life and Times of Fanny Hill* (Bristol Old Vic). Other credits include *Il Trittico, Flight, Madame Butterfly, La Fanciulla* (Opera Holland Park) and *Projet Polunin* (Sadler's Wells).

George Dennis Sound Design and Composition

George's theatre credits include *The Homecoming* (Trafalgar Studios; Olivier Award nomination), *The Pitchfork Disney, Killer* (Shoreditch Town Hall), *The Convert, In the Night Time, Image of an Unknown Young Woman, Eclipsed, The Edge of our Bodies* (Gate Theatre), *Harrogate* (HighTide Festival and Royal Court), *Fireworks, Liberian Girl, Primetime* (Royal Court), *The Mountaintop, The Island* (Young Vic), *Imogen, The Taming of the Shrew* (Shakespeare's Globe), *In Fidelity* (Traverse/HighTide Festival), *Noises Off* (Nottingham Playhouse/ Northern Stage/Nuffield Southampton), *German Skerries* (Orange Tree), *Brave New World, Regeneration* (Royal and Derngate/Touring Consortium), *Forget Me Not, Visitors* (Bush Theatre), *Eventide* (Arcola Theatre/UK Tour), *Chicken* (Eastern Angles/Unity Theatre), *Beautiful Thing* (Arts Theatre/UK Tour),

A Breakfast of Eels, *The Last Yankee* (Print Room), *peddling* (Arcola Theatre/59E59, New York/HighTide Festival), *Mametz* (National Theatre of Wales), *Minotaur* (Polka Theatre/Clwyd Theatr Cymru), *Spring Awakening* (Headlong), *Love Your Soldiers* (Sheffield Crucible Studio), *Thark* (Park Theatre), *Moth* (Bush Theatre/HighTide Festival), *Hello/Goodbye* (Hampstead Theatre) and *Liar Liar* (Unicorn Theatre).

Kate Waters Fight Director

Kate is one of only two women on the Equity Register of Fight Directors. Her theatre credits include *Disgraced* (Bush Theatre), *Othello*, *As You Like It*, *Our Country's Good*, *Rules For Living*, *Dara*, *Hotel*, *The Curious Incident of the Dog in the Night-Time*, *War Horse* (National Theatre), *Hand to God (West End)*, *The Last Goodbye* (The Old Globe, San Diego, California), *Dr Faustus*, *The Maids*, *Macbeth*, *Richard III*, *East Is East*, *The Ruling Class*, *The Hothouse*, *The Pride* (Jamie Lloyd Company), *A Midsummer Night's Dream*, *Merchant of Venice*, *Anthony & Cleopatra*, *Dr Faustus* (The Globe), *Liberian Girl* (Royal Court), *Black Comedy* (Chichester Festival Theatre), *Urinetown The Musical* (St James Theatre and West End), *Don Giovanni* (ROH), *Bugsy Malone* and *Herons* (Lyric Hammersmith). Kate is a regular fight director for *Coronation Street*, *Emmerdale* and *Hollyoaks*.

Lydia Crimp Costume Supervisor

Lydia trained in Fashion Design at The University for the Creative Arts before taking on full time roles as Production Coordinator at Academy Costumes and later as a costume buyer at the National Theatre. Since then, Lydia's work as Costume Supervisor for the National Theatre includes *The Curious Incident of the Dog in the Night time* (West End and Broadway), *People* (UK Tour), *Cocktail Sticks* (West End), *Evening at the Talk House, Les Blancs* and *Love*. Other work includes *Fireworks* (Royal Court), *The Maids* (Trafalgar Studios), *This House* (Chichester Festival Theatre, Garrick Theatre) and *My Brilliant Friend* at The Rose Theatre. Lydia is also a keen portrait artist.

Homer Simpson Productions Associate Producers
Sally Homer and Zoë Simpson met in the late 90s whilst working
at Theatre Royal Stratford East. Zoë was Associate Producer at
David Ian Productions and recently produced *The Man Jesus* by
Matthew Hurt starring Simon Callow on tour. Sally has had a long
career in live performance publicity and marketing. Together
they produced *The Dylathon* (to mark Dylan Thomas' centenary
celebrations in 2014) and UK tours of *The Amazing Bubble Man*
(2015) and the radical Dutch comedian *Hans Teeuwen* (2016).
They are currently planning multiple UK productions in 2018
of Dougal Irvine's *Angry Birds*, a new punk musical for young
people about the suffragettes and are also developing a musical
about the women who wrote with Bertolt Brecht entitled *Brecht's
Threepenny Bits.*

Bush Theatre

Bush Theatre

We make theatre for London. Now.

The Bush is a world-famous home for new plays and an internationally renowned champion of playwrights. We discover, nurture and produce the best new writers from the widest range of backgrounds from our home in a distinctive corner of west London.

The Bush has won over 100 awards and developed an enviable reputation for touring its acclaimed productions nationally and internationally.

We are excited by exceptional new voices, stories and perspectives – particularly those with contemporary bite which reflect the vibrancy of British culture now.

Located in the newly renovated old library on Uxbridge Road in the heart of Shepherd's Bush, the theatre houses two performance spaces, a rehearsal room and the lively Library Bar.

 Supported by ARTS COUNCIL ENGLAND h&f hammersmith & fulham

bushtheatre.co.uk

THANK YOU
TO OUR SUPPORTERS

The Bush Theatre would like to thank all its supporters whose valuable contributions have helped us to create a platform for our future and to promote the highest quality new writing, develop the next generation of creative talent and lead innovative community engagement work.

LONE STAR

Eric Abraham
Gianni Alen-Buckley
Michael Alen-Buckley
Rafael & Anne-Helene Biosse Duplan
Garvin & Steffanie Brown
Rob & Siri Cope
Miles Morland

HANDFUL OF STARS

Dawn & Gary Baker
Sofia Barattieri
Martin Bartle
Richard & Lucille Briance
Charlie Bigham
Clive & Helena Butler
Clare & Chris Clark
Clyde Cooper
Alice Findlay
Zarina Funk
Richard & Jane Gordon
Vera Monotti Graziadei
Madeleine Hodgkin
Priscilla John
Simon & Katherine Johnson
Philippa Seal & Philip Jones QC
V&F Lukey
Georgia Oetker
Philip & Biddy Percival
Robert Rooney
Joana & Henrik Schliemann
Lesley Hill & Russ Shaw
Team Nelson
and one anonymous donor.

RISING STARS

ACT IV
Nicholas Alt
Mark Bentley
David Brooks
Simon Burstein
Matthew Byam Shaw
Jennifer Caruso Viall
Tim & Andrea Clark
Sarah Clarke
Claude & Susie Cochin de Billy
Lois Cox
Matthew Cushen
Andrew & Amanda Duncan
Natalie Fellowes & Simon Gresham Jones
Lady Antonia Fraser
Jack Gordon & Kate Lacy
Hugh & Sarah Grootenhuis

RISING STARS CONTINUED

Thea Guest
Mary Harvey
Ann & Ravi Joseph
Davina & Malcolm Judelson
Cathy & Paul Kafka
Miggy Littlejohns
Isabella Macpherson
Liz & Luke Mayhew
Michael McCoy
Judith Mellor
Caro Millington
Mark & Anne Paterson
Barbara Prideaux
Emily Reeve
Renske & Marion
Sarah Richards
Sophie Silocchi
Susie Saville Sneath
Saleem & Alexandra Siddiqi
Brian Smith
Nick Starr
Peter Tausig
Lady Marina Vaizey
Guy Vincent & Sarah Mitchell
Amanda Waggott
Sir Robert & Lady Wilson
Peter Wilson-Smith & Kat Callo
Alison Winter
and three anonymous donors.

SPONSORS & SUPPORTERS

AKA
Alen-Buckley LLP
Gianni & Michael Alen-Buckley
Jeremy Attard Manche
Bill & Judy Bollinger
Edward Bonham Carter
Martin Bowley
Duke & Duchess of Buccleuch
The Hon Mrs Louise Burness
Sir Charles & Lady Isabella Burrell
Philip & Tita Byrne
CHK Charities Limited
Peppe & Quentin Ciardi
Joanna & Hadyn Cunningham
Leo & Grega Daly
Patrick & Mairead Flaherty
Sue Fletcher
The Hon Sir Rocco Forte
The Hon Portia Forte
Mark Franklin
The Right Hon Piers Gibson
Farid & Emille Gragour
Victoria Gray
John Gordon

SPONSORS & SUPPORTERS CONTINUED

Vivienne Guinness
Melanie Hall
Lesley Hill & Russ Shaw
Madeleine Hodgkin
Michael Holland & Denise O'Donoghue
Graham & Amanda Hutton
James Gorst Architects Ltd.
Simon & Katherine Johnson
Bernard Lambilliotte
The Lord Forte Foundation
Peter & Bettina Mallinson
Mahoro Charitable Trust
Mitsui Fodosan (U.K.) Ltd
Alfred Munkenbeck III
Nick Hern Books
RAB Capital
Josie Rourke
Kevin Pakenham
Tim & Catherine Score
Search Foundation
Richard Sharp
Susie Simkins
Edward Snape & Marilyn Eardley
Michael & Sarah Spencer
Stanhope PLC
Ross Turner
The Syder Foundation
van Tulleken Family
Johnny & Dione Verulam
Robert & Felicity Waley-Cohen
Westfield London
Phillip Wooller
Danny Wyler
and three anonymous donors.

TRUSTS AND FOUNDATIONS

The Andrew Lloyd Webber Foundation
The Druce Wake Charitable Trust
The City Bridge Trust
Cockayne—Grants for the Arts
The John S Cohen Foundation
The Daisy Trust
The Equity Charitable Trust
Eranda Rothschild Foundation
Esmée Fairbairn Foundation
Fidelio Charitable Trust
Foyle Foundation
Garfield Weston Foundation
Garrick Charitable Trust

TRUSTS AND FOUNDATIONS CONTINUED

The Gatsby Charitable Foundation
The Harold Hyam Wingate Foundation
Hammersmith United Charities
Heritage of London Trust
The Idlewild Trust
John Lyon's Charity
The J Paul Getty Jnr Charitable Trust
The John Thaw Foundation
The Leche Trust
The Leverhulme Trust
The London Community Foundation
Margaret Guido's Charitable Trust
The Martin Bowley Charitable Trust
The Monument Trust
Paul Hamlyn Foundation
Pilgrim Trust
The Theatres Trust
Viridor Credits
The Williams Charitable Trust
Western Riverside Environmental Fund
The Wolfson Foundation
and one anonymous donor.

CORPORATE SPONSORS & MEMBERS

The Agency (London) Ltd
Dorsett Shepherds Bush
Drama Centre London
The Groucho Club
THE HOXTON

PUBLIC FUNDING

If you are interested in finding out how to be involved, please visit the 'Support Us' section of bushtheatre.co.uk or email **development@bushtheatre.co.uk** or call **020 8743 3584**

GUARDS AT THE TAJ

Rajiv Joseph

GUARDS AT THE TAJ

OBERON BOOKS
LONDON

WWW.OBERONBOOKS.COM

First published in 2016 as *Guards at the Taj and Mr. Wolf: Two Plays* by Soft Skull, an imprint of Counterpoint Press.

This edition first published in 2017 by Oberon Books Ltd
521 Caledonian Road, London N7 9RH
Tel: +44 (0.) 20 7607 3637 / Fax: +44 (0.) 20 7607 3629
e-mail: info@oberonbooks.com
www.oberonbooks.com

A catalogue record for this book is available from the British Library.

PB ISBN: 9781786821430
E ISBN: 9781786821447

Cover design by

Visit www.oberonbooks.com to read more about all our books and to buy them. You will also find features, author interviews and news of any author events, and you can sign up for e-newsletters so that you're always first to hear about our new releases.

Characters

HUMAYUN

BABUR

Time: 1648

Place: Agra, India

Note: Actors should not use a dialect.

SCENE 1

Agra, India. 1648. Night. HUMAYUN, a young Imperial Guard, stands watch.

Brilliant stars dot the sky, but there is no moon. Crickets chirp. The distant call of a crazed bird. Otherwise silence.

Another guard, BABUR, hurriedly enters, very much disheveled, late to his post.

He awkwardly sets up in guard position a few feet away from HUMAYUN, trying to get properly dressed. HUMAYUN doesn't move – but he's clearly irritated by BABUR.

Finally BABUR is set. He stands at attention like HUMAYUN.

HUMAYUN: Wrong hand.

> *BABUR switches his sword to the proper hand, holding the blade perfectly upright, against his body.*
>
> *A long beat. They stand guard. Crickets. The same crazy bird calls out. Aaarixah!*

BABUR: *(Imitates.) Aaarixah!*

HUMAYUN: *Shhhh!*

BABUR: Which one is that?

HUMAYUN: *Shhhh!*

> *Crazed bird again. Aaarixah!*

BABUR: I don't know them like you know them. The birds. Which bird is that one? Chickadee? Sandgrouse? Thick-knee?

HUMAYUN: Shut up!

BABUR: You always know the birds, I don't know any birds or –

HUMAYUN: Would you be quiet!?

BABUR: I'm just saying…

HUMAYUN: "Imperial Guards of the Great Walled City of Agra, Sworn to the Eternal Dominion of His Most Supreme Benevolence Emperor Shah Jahan… *Do Not Speak.*"

BABUR: You just spoke.

HUMAYUN: "Among the Sacred Oaths of the Mughal Imperial Guard is to *Never Speak.*"

BABUR: You keep talking about not talking.

HUMAYUN: "In silence, we are vigilant."

BABUR: Swearing an Oath to Not Speak: *Contradiction!*

HUMAYUN: Babur! Stop! You have to be careful!

BABUR: Okay!

HUMAYUN: I'm serious!

BABUR: Okay.

HUMAYUN: They'll release us from this Honored Fleet without a second thought! The tiniest of infractions will see us both gone; quick-stuffed to the lowliest gullies of Agra.

BABUR: You won't tell on me.

HUMAYUN: Well, I won't lie.

BABUR: Come on! We're brothers, you and me.

HUMAYUN: We're not brothers, we're just friends.

BABUR: That's insensitive. That makes me sad. I think of you as a brother. As a bhai. You call me bhai. I call you bhai.

HUMAYUN: Don't make me lose my job.

BABUR: Hah! You?! And who is your father? Only simply the highest of high command in the All-On-High Imperial Guard.

HUMAYAN: My father yearns for my defeat. Always has. You know him.

BABUR: Sons are sons. Fathers are Fathers. And one day you'll be Chief Top Boss Man of the Imperial Guard just like him.

HUMAYUN: That will never happen. He thinks I'm soft. Stop talking. Stand guard.

Beat. Other bird sounds. Then quiet.

BABUR: You know what I wonder about?

HUMAYUN: No. Shut up.

BABUR: I was wondering... When will we get to guard the Imperial Harem?

HUMAYUN: Ha.

BABUR: I'm serious, when?

HUMAYUN: Guards of the Imperial Harem are tip-top guards. Seniority. Best position in the fleet. We are not tip-top. We get the Dawn Watch. We'll both be grey and toothless before they let us guard the Harem.

BABUR: But your father... maybe he could...

HUMAYUN: That will never happen.

BABUR: Never?

HUMAYUN: Absolutely never.

> *Beat.*

BABUR: Man, I want to see the Harem.

HUMAYUN: It's supposed to be pretty boring.

BABUR: *(Skeptical.) Really.*

HUMAYUN: It's not so salacious a venue as the gossip would have you think.

BABUR: It's a *Harem.*

HUMAYUN: It's a government department, like any other office. It's where the emperor does his most confidential work. Thus, only the Mahaldar, the concubines and eunuchs are allowed within the walls... and the two most trusted Imperial Guards who are, decidedly, *not us.*

BABUR: *(Marveling.)* But I mean... Surrounded by naked women!

HUMAYAN: It's not like that!

BABUR: Okay.

HUMAYUN: It's not some depraved house of sluts!

BABUR: Okay.

HUMAYUN: It's not some hotbed of wanton lust!

BABUR: *Okay.*

HUMAYUN: It's just... You know... A place the emperor goes... to work.

> *(Beat; both guys imagine what goes on in the Harem.)*
>
> *(HUMAYUN clears his throat.)*

Let's stand guard.

BABUR: Okay.

> *They stand guard. BABUR starts thrusting his pelvis, slowly, but gaining in force and eros.*

BABUR: Harem... Duty... Harem... Duty...

HUMAYUN: Stop. STOP! Babur, that's messed up, man, stop it!

> *BABUR stops.*

BABUR: I want to see that Harem before I die.

HUMAYUN: Well, you can improve your chances by showing up on time and shutting your seditious mouth.

BABUR: "Seditious?"

HUMAYUN: You heard me.

BABUR: How is that *seditious?*

HUMAYUN: It just is.

BABUR: I was making a joke.

HUMAYUN: Mild Sedition.

BABUR: *Mild?* According to who?

HUMAYUN: According to the King! If you had paid attention in training, you would know that sedition is recognized at three levels in accordance with his most supreme and benevolent monarch. You just made a humorous commentary at the expense of the King's most beloved bureaucratic office. Punishment for Mild Sedition: forty lashes with a whip and a shaved head.

HUMAYUN: Yes. And Medium Sedition carries a sentence of blinding. Extreme Sedition: Being sown into the hide of a water buffalo and left in the sun for seven days. And in the case of Treason: Death by Elephant. All of which is to say, Babur, *shut up*. Imperial Guards are Not To Speak!

BABUR: Okay!

> *They stand guard. The crazed bird calls out again, although maybe a little less crazed. Aaarixah…*

HUMAYUN: Red-breasted jibjab. That's what it is. The bird.

BABUR: Ah! You're good, Huma.

HUMAYUN: Now please. Quiet.

> *Long beat.*

BABUR: Huma? Do you ever wonder…

HUMAYUN: No.

BABUR: All these celestial luminations that mark our sky…

HUMAYUN: What of them?

BABUR: The stars: What are they?

HUMAYUN: Determinations of our fates and futures.

BABUR: But what ARE they?

Are they like fires in the distance? And if so, if you get closer to them, do they become, you know, brighter and hotter? And if so, how far away are they exactly? In the mountains you can determine the closeness of a point, but in the sky, there are no such methods of orientation.

> *(Long beat.)*

Humayun.
Humayun.

Humayun.

Humayun.

HUMAYUN: WHAT?

BABUR: One day? Thousands of years from now? I bet there will be a sort of palanquin that can soar into the stars like some giant bird.

HUMAYUN: A giant palanquin bird.

BABUR: Yeah.

HUMAYUN: Palanquins are for women.

BABUR: Not this one. This one will be for everyone.

Except, rather than men, or elephants, this will be carried by some unfound-as-of-yet force – up to the stars! And in this palanquin, one might track those little fires in the sky.

HUMAYUN: You and your fantasies.

BABUR: Not fantasies; predictions. And you like them. You've always liked them.

HUMAYUN: Fairy tales for children. Not Imperial Guards.

BABUR: And this flying palanquin will be fast. Faster than any horse, or any bird. *Tuff-tuff! Tuff-tuff! Fast!* You understand, Huma? And, so, *tuff-tuff,* you will be able to get closer to those fires in the sky.

HUMAYUN: And then?

BABUR: They must be leading us somewhere. If they are determinations of our fates, then they must be arranged by some grand conspirator.

HUMAYUN: Allah.

BABUR: Yeah. Allah.

HUMAYUN: Allahu Akbar.

BABUR: Yeah.
Sure.
But something else, too, right?

HUMAYUN: Blasphemy. Come on, don't say that.

BABUR: It's only something I wonder about.

HUMAYUN: It's not meant for us to know.

BABUR: But maybe it is! If there is something to see, and therefore, something to think about, and therefore something to wonder about... then there's something to go towards.

HUMAYUN: Like a moth to a candle or a tiger to a trap.

BABUR: No.

HUMAYUN: Then what.

BABUR: I think God wants us to learn more and more things. I mean...
Look what is about to be revealed behind us!

HUMAYUN: No. Don't. Don't look. Imperial Guards are Not to Move.

BABUR: They say it will be the most beautiful thing in the world.

HUMAYUN: Yes, well, His Supreme Highness has specified that it *should* be, and so it *will* be.

BABUR: What do you think it will look like?

> *Beat.*

HUMAYUN: They say it's white.

BABUR: Yeah, but just white? Is it skinny? Is it fat? I mean, what shape will it be? All we know are those protective walls that have hidden it these past sixteen years.

HUMAYUN: The city within the city.

BABUR: It's crazy! Sixteen years in the making! Since we were kids, they've been building this! And yet we have no idea what it will look like! Because within the walls, where Tajmahal is built: Another city, a secret one, with strange men who have lived a different life than anyone else!

HUMAYUN: His most supreme emperor Shah Jahan decreed that no one shall see it until it is fully completed.

BABUR: But *why?*

HUMAYUN: There need not be a reason, it is a royal decree! *The construction of Tajmahal is not to be seen by anyone except the masons, laborers and slaves who exist within those walls.*

BABUR: And the architect.
(With great reverence.) Ustad Isa.

HUMAYUN: *(With less reverence.)* Ustad Isa.

BABUR: *Ustad Isa.* They say he is the smartest man in the kingdom. In any kingdom. The smartest man on earth.

HUMAYUN: *(With disdain.)* Doubtful.

BABUR: He speaks to the King. He looks the king in the eye. He is equal to the King.

HUMAYUN: That is mild-to-medium sedition.

BABUR: But then he drinks with the masons. And he frequents the whores. He built a school for the peasant children on his day off.

HUMAYUN: I saw it, it was too big.

BABUR: He smiles at everyone! Can you imagine such a thing? Smiling at *every person.*

The happiest man in the world.

HUMAYUN: The happiest man in the world is also the craziest. Behead that man. Kick his skull to the dogs. Let them play with it, as dogs do.

BABUR: Do you know why he's the happiest?

HUMAYUN: I just said.

BABUR: Do you remember that thing we made in the trees? First year in the army.

HUMAYUN: Our platform.

BABUR: We were three nights in the woods, afraid of tigers.
It was like floating in the branches, high above the jungle!
We used our swords to smoothen the wood. Cut it so it
fit together. Smooth, clean ledge! Some of the wood was
sandalwood. The scent of it cloaked us through the night,
protecting us from mosquitoes. Ahhh! The rough perfume
of sandalwood!

HUMAYUN: I have never slept as soundly as I slept on that raft
we made in the trees.

BABUR: Do you remember how good it felt when we had
completed it? Sitting, admiring it, bathed in sweat, drinking
cold riverwater.

HUMAYUN: Yes.

BABUR: Now: Think how Ustad Isa must feel. Sixteen years in
the making, surrounded by those walls, so that no one may
see it until it is complete…

HUMAYUN: Which is today's first light.

BABUR: Which is today's first light. And for sixteen years, he
built this thing.
He smiles at everyone, because he is happy. Because he
made Tajmahal. Ustad Isa is amazing! Even God couldn't
make Tajmahal!

HUMAYUN: Blasphemy! Would you stop? Don't forget the
punishment for blasphemy is three days in prison.

BABUR: That is weird, though, isn't it?

HUMAYUN: What?

BABUR: Mild sedition – for example, making a joke! – is…
whipping, shaved head, *torture*… but *blasphemy*… just three
days in jail! As if the emperor doesn't *really* care about
speaking ill of Allah. He's way more concerned about himself.

HUMAYUN: Don't test him! And stop with this Ustad Isa talk.
Tajmahal was made by His Sovereign Ruler of Hindustan,
Shah Jahan who built this for his tragic queen, Her

Excellent Empress Mumtaz Mahal. This is her tomb, a mausoleum to honor her for all time.

BABUR: Nah.

HUMAYUN: Nah what?!

BABUR: Ustad Isa. He made Tajmahal.

HUMAYUN: Oh yeah? Did Ustad Isa import the Pietra Dura from Greece? Or the Herringbone from Iraq? Or the Marble from China? Or 700 tons of Jasper from some damnfool slum in Uzbekistan!? No: He didn't. Shah Jahan did.

BABUR: Ustad Isa says that today's first light is important for Tajmahal because *after* today, the air and the rain and the sand and heat of sun will start to age her perfect face. But that today, at first light, Tajmahal will be the most beautiful thing in the history of everything that has *ever existed*.

> *(Beat.)*

Think about it! The most beautiful thing ever made… Tajmahal is sitting there, waiting to be lit by the day's first light… waiting to be seen –

HUMAYUN: We are <u>not</u> turning around.

BABUR: AW, COME ON MAN!

HUMAYUN: No. We are guarding. We are facing South. Not North. South.

BABUR: Just for a quick moment! We turn around, we turn back around…

HUMAYUN: Absolutely not. Imperial Guards do not move from their post.

BABUR: They don't speak either, but here we are / speaking for a long…

HUMAYUN: We're not turning around! We are Imperial Guards! This is very important to me!

BABUR: To me as well. But…

HUMAYUN: People are watching us.

BABUR: Who?

HUMAYUN: Elders. Waiting for us to deviate from the sacred oaths. You and me, Babur, there is no one below us. If there is a post that nobody wants? For example the one single guard post that faces AWAY from Tajmahal at dawn? Then we are assigned that post.

We are grunts of the Imperial Force until that day new appointments are made. And until that day: *We get the jobs nobody else wants.*

Unless, of course, we are sacked for being stupid because we turned around at first light to see a white building. They'd send us to the brink.

We'd end up patrolling Kashmir – a place to which, if some bastard is assigned, some bastard ends up dead.

> *(Beat.)*

Do you want to go patrol Kashmir?

BABUR: No.

HUMAYUN: Do you want forty lashes and a shaved head?

BABUR: No.

HUMAYUN: Do you want to be blinded by a dull blade? Or sewn into the hide of a water buffalo?

BABUR: No.

HUMAYUN: Or maybe you want to end up like poor Ustad Isa and…

> *HUMAYUN cuts off. BABUR notices.*

BABUR: Wait, what?

HUMAYUN: Nothing.

BABUR: No, what were you just saying?

HUMAYUN: Nothing. Forget it.

BABUR: What about Ustad Isa?

HUMAYUN: Nothing…

BABUR: Come on, what?

HUMAYUN: Nothing.

BABUR: Humayun.

HUMAYUN: No.

BABUR: Huma…

HUMAYUN: No.

BABUR: Tell me.

HUMAYUN: No.

BABUR: What have you heard.

HUMAYUN: It's simple: Don't be careless.

> *Beat.*

BABUR: Come on. Tell me.

HUMAYUN: Okay. But you can't tell anyone.

BABUR: I promise! Who keeps a promise better than me?

HUMAYUN: Okay.

It has been said, that after the last jewels were inlaid, and the last piece of marble polished… it has been said that this wastrel, this cur, Ustad Isa, the proud architect who thinks himself equal to a King, approached Shah Jahan himself and asked His Excellent Mughal Lineage for a *personal* favor.

BABUR: A *personal* favor?

HUMAYUN: Yes.

BABUR: He asked the Emperor for a Personal Favor?

HUMAYUN: *(Almost delighted by this.)* I don't even know which level of sedition that is because it's never been classified because nobody's ever done it! This is the kind of useless vagabond your brilliant artist is. He asks Shah Jahan, great great grandson of Babur, First Mughal Emperor –

BABUR: – My namesake

HUMAYUN: – Your namesake – Ustad Isa asks Shah Jahan for things such as these, personal things.

BABUR: My God.

HUMAYUN: Yes.

> *Beat.*

BABUR: What was it?

HUMAYUN: *(As if telling a secret.)* Ustad Isa asked Shah Jahan if the 20,000 men who built it, could wander the unsheathed Tajmahal at first light, so that they could see and admire their handiwork, this thing to which they owe the last sixteen years of their lives.

BABUR: Oh.
Huh.
What did Shah Jahan reply?

HUMAYUN: His Supreme Excellent Imperious Royalty said No.

BABUR: Oh.

HUMAYUN: But there is a rumor.

BABUR: Of?

HUMAYUN: Having never in his life been asked a personal favor before – His Most Sovereign Enlightened One needed time to fully *absorb* the gross insult hurled upon him.

BABUR: The Emperor is angry.

HUMAYUN: Yeah. The Emperor is angry. So now the emperor has issued a decree: Nothing so beautiful as Tajmahal shall ever be built again.

BABUR: What kind of decree is *that?*

HUMAYUN: He has ordered that the hands of every mason, laborer and artisan who crafted Tajmahal… be chopped off.

BABUR: WHAT?

Wait wait wait. He's going to chop 20,000 hands off?

HUMAYUN: 40,000.

BABUR: Because they wanted to look at Tajmahal?

HUMAYUN: We need not ask why. A Royal Decree is exactly that.

BABUR: Every worker? Every man who built this?

HUMAYUN: Every one.

BABUR: So someone is going to have to chop off 40,000 hands?

HUMAYUN: Yep.

BABUR: That's a terrible job. Who's gonna have to do that?

A long beat as they both realize what this means.

HUMAYUN: Shit.

BABUR: Oh no…

HUMAYUN: Shit.

BABUR: It's us, right?

HUMAYUN: Shit.

BABUR: I don't want to do that!

HUMAYUN: I don't either.

BABUR: Shit.

Beat.

BABUR: Well, I think the Emperor is overreacting.

Beat.

BABUR: 40,000 severed hands. What's the purpose of such punishment?

HUMAYUN: *Nothing so beautiful as Tajmahal shall ever be built again.*

This news depresses BABUR. Also HUMAYUN, although he wouldn't admit it. Long Beat. BABUR looks at the stars.

BABUR: It's almost first light.

(Beat.)

Huma…

HUMAYUN: What.

BABUR: If a flying palanquin did exist, like the one I said… and a person could fly to those little fires in the sky… would you go?

HUMAYUN: If it pleased His All-Powerful Reign.

BABUR: I would go, even if it didn't please him. What an invention that would be!

I would call it… an Allah-aero-platforma-al-Agra-Babura… Or for short… Aeroplat.

HUMAYUN: *Aeroplat.*

BABUR: Can you imagine? To be as far away as that? Agra would seem no bigger than the flickering up there.

We are as small as that, Huma.

And further away from that, we are smaller.

And further away from that… we don't exist. There is no proof of us, or this place, of Tajmahal, or Shah Jahan or Hindustan, or the razai of candlelight above our heads.

Far enough away… is another world, with different Kings, and different Imperial Guards.

Different Gods, even.

A beat. Then BABUR turns around to look at the Taj.

HUMAYUN: *(Panicking, but not moving.)*

Babur, what are you doing?

Turn back around! You… you can't… Babur!

As BABUR starts to really see the Taj, the Taj also transforms, each passing moment slowly bringing a new shade of morning light.

BABUR: Humayun.

HUMAYUN: Turn around!

BABUR: Humayun.

HUMAYUN: Babur, if anyone sees you…

BABUR: Humayun!

HUMAYUN: *Why are you doing this, man!?*

BABUR: I think you should look.

HUMAYUN: We can look at any other time! Any other time except now! Why is it so important to risk everything to look at this now! Turn around!

>*With each second, BABUR is more transformed. A new light shines on the Taj. He lowers his sword, as if it had simply become too heavy.*

HUMAYUN: Babur! Raise your sword!

>*BABUR drops his sword to the ground. Involuntarily. He doesn't even know he has done it.*

HUMAYUN: You dropped your… Oh COME ON man! You are an *Imperial Guard.* They will…

BABUR: There's no one watching. Not us, Huma. Trust me. There are no eyes in this land that would waste themselves on us. They are not watching us. They are watching this. This. Huma-bhai… Look. Look and see…

>*HUMAYUN finally breaks, a little, and very slowly, awkwardly turns around. He stares at the Taj. Both men do.*

>*After a moment, and another shift of morning light, HUMAYUN lowers his sword. Eventually he drops his sword, too.*

>*Both men, without sound, and without even knowing, begin to weep.*

>*They are experiencing Awe in the most biblical sense. It is Fear, it is one of the fires in the sky, landed in their city.*

HUMAYUN hits BABUR's arm and holds on to it, as if to make sure they both aren't dreaming.

HUMAYUN's clutch of BABUR's arm slowly loosens, drops.

The two men, as if to keep themselves slightly in reality, take each other's hands. They hold hands and watch the first light of day illuminate the Taj Mahal.

SCENE 2

Lights up on a far away underground chamber.

The floor is pooled with blood. Smoke is in the air. There are several giant baskets that are heavy with blood and severed hands.

There is a waist-high wooden chopping block, like a podium, particularly soaked with blood.

HUMAYUN lies on a bench, his eyes shut. He holds a smoking cauterizing iron.

BABUR sits in the corner, slumped over, almost as if in a trance. He grips a large sword tightly with both hands. The sword, his hands, his arms, his entire body – soaked with blood.

Neither man moves for a long time.

Finally, HUMAYUN, as if waking from a dream, sits up, drops the iron, and rubs his eyes. Looks. Rubs his eyes some more… He can't see…

HUMAYUN: Babur. Babur. Babur… BABUR!

BABUR: What.

HUMAYUN: I can't see.

BABUR: What?

HUMAYUN: I can't see.

BABUR: What do you mean you can't see.

HUMAYUN: I mean, I am opening my eyes and I can't see! I'm blind!

BABUR: What are you talking about?

23

HUMAYUN: I'm fucking blind!

BABUR: You're not blind.

HUMAYUN: I'M BLIND, I'M TELLING YOU.

BABUR: You probably just got smoke in them.

HUMAYUN: Smoke doesn't make you go blind!

BABUR: You just cauterized 40,000 stumps! You were seeing just fine then!

HUMAYUN: I know, but NOW I CAN'T SEE!

HUMAYUN walks around blindly, looking for something.

HUMAYUN: I need water… I need to wash out my eyes. Babur, get the water.. find it and bring it to me. BABUR!

BABUR: Okay, I'll get the water…

BABUR stands up, still clutching his sword. He suddenly realizes he can't let go of the sword.

BABUR: Huma… HUMA!!

HUMAYUN: What?

BABUR: My HANDS!

HUMAYUN: What about them?!

BABUR: I can't let go… I can't let go… They're stuck… I CAN'T LET GO OF MY SWORD!

HUMAYUN: You're just cramped. Relax –

BABUR: I CAN'T LET GO OF MY HANDS!

HUMAYUN: JUST RELAX!

BABUR: Don't tell me to relax!

HUMAYUN: Your hands are just cramped! From all the chopping! Relax and you can –

BABUR: Don't tell me to relax!

HUMAYUN: I'm *blind* okay?

BABUR: You're not blind.

HUMAYUN: I can't see!

BABUR: I can't get you water until my hands uncramp.

HUMAYUN: Well un-cramp them!

BABUR: I don't know how to uncramp them!

HUMAYUN: Massage them!

BABUR: With what? My feet!?

HUMAYUN: Figure something out I need the god damn water for my eyes, I CAN'T SEE!

BABUR: Okay, okay, okay… just…

HUMAYUN: Come on, Babur…

BABUR: If you massage my hands, and get this sword out of my hands, I'll get you water, okay? Okay, Huma?

HUMAYUN: Where are you?

BABUR: Here.

HUMAYUN: *Where* "here"?

BABUR: Here!

HUMAYUN: Am I walking towards you?

BABUR: No, turn around.

HUMAYUN: Now?

BABUR: No, turn halfway around!

The other halfway! Follow my voice!

HUMAYUN: It echoes in here! You sound like you're everywhere. *(Panics.) I'm fucking blind!*

BABUR: There now step towards me and I'll step towards you, but don't step into my sword, okay, because it's sticking straight out…

> *HUMAYUN, cautiously walks towards BABUR... but then slips in a pool of blood. This causes BABUR also to slip in a pool of blood.*

> *... they both splash to the floor, and then both scramble to get up, and both slip again, effectively covering themselves in more blood. The slipping and sliding causes both of them to panic even more.*

BABUR: STOP IT! Don't move! Don't move! I'll move towards you...

> *BABUR slides on his butt over to HUMAYUN (both of them drenched, head to toe, in blood).*

BABUR: Careful of my sword.

HUMAYUN: Okay.

BABUR: Here are my hands. Okay.

HUMAYUN: They're like stone.

BABUR: I know, I told you.

HUMAYUN: Relax them.

BABUR: I'm trying.

> *HUMAYUN massages BABUR's hands.*

HUMAYUN: God.

BABUR: I know.

HUMAYUN: What just happened?

BABUR: I don't know.

20,000 men. 40,000 hands.

HUMAYUN: I can't believe we chopped off 40,000 hands.

BABUR: NO.

HUMAYUN: No what?

BABUR: *I* cut off 40,000. You cauterized. I chopped, you cauterized.

HUMAYUN: So?

BABUR: Different!

HUMAYUN: Both unsavory.

BABUR: Different!

HUMAYUN: How's it different?

BABUR: I took apart, you put together.

HUMAYUN: We could have switched! You think I was having a party over there, cauterizing stumps? I went blind!

BABUR: You're not blind!

HUMAYUN: You get cramps in your hands, I go blind, who had the worse job? Answer me that, fucko.

BABUR: IT WAS DIFFERENT. I chopped off hands. And then, instead of bleeding to death, you stopped the bleeding. I caused damage that you then healed. How do you not see the difference in these things?! How do you not see that?

HUMAYUN: *Because I'm blind!*

BABUR: Just massage my hands so I can get you water so I can stop hearing about how blind you are.

HUMAYUN: I'm trying.

BABUR: Try harder.

> *More massaging.*

BABUR: Chopping was worse.

HUMAYUN: We could have switched.

BABUR: But we couldn't! We fell into a rhythm!

HUMAYUN: We fell into a trance. I don't even remember. It's like I don't even remember doing it.

BABUR: I do.

They continue this, almost silently, as HUMAYUN massages BABUR's hands.

HUMAYUN: You know that uh…
That invention you had? The… uh…

(Thinks, trying to remember.)

Allaporta-palanquin-pa? Or… was that it?

BABUR: Aeroplat.

HUMAYUN: The thing that could fly to the stars?
That was a good idea.

(Beat.)

But I was wondering… what if you fell off? If this mechanism was soaring to the stars, like some giant bird with cushions… wouldn't one be in danger of being swept away by the wind, or maybe in an effort to see the everything below, the palaces and streets and jungles, wouldn't, curiosity, couldn't it, somehow, make a curious person peer too far over the edge of his flying box and then plummet down and then Splatooey?

BABUR: There would be a strap.

HUMAYUN: A strap?

BABUR: Attached to the sitting cushion. Wrapping around the stomach like a belt.

HUMYAUN: Some kind of Seat-Belt.

BABUR: Yes.

HUMAYUN: That's a good idea.

BABUR: Yeah. *Ahhhhhhh….*

BABUR's hands finally loosen. HUMAYUN pries the sword away, tosses it to the side.

HUMAYUN: There you go… now, please get me some water?

BABUR gets up, goes over to a clay urn and gets a large cup of water and brings it back to HUMAYUN. He pours water slowly over HUMAYUN's face, while HUMAYUN rubs his eyes.

BABUR: I don't know why water's going to make you see.

HUMAYUN: I just need something… Ahhh… God… More water, MORE WATER!

BABUR rushes back, gets more water, brings it back to HUMAYUN. He rinses his eyes out more, squints, opens them wide looks around.

BABUR: Can you see?

HUMAYUN: *(With joy.)* I can… I can!

BABUR: Look at me. You can see me?

HUMAYUN: *(In seeing BABUR, soaked in blood, is horrified.)* I can see you…

HUMAYUN looks around at the room, covered in blood. He gets to his feet.

HUMAYUN: Whoa.

BABUR: Yeah.

HUMAYUN: What a mess.

BABUR: Yeah.

HUMAYUN: We have to clean this ourselves?

BABUR: Yeah.

HUMAYUN: This is woman's work.

BABUR: I know.

HUMAYUN: There should literally be twenty women in here cleaning this right now.

BABUR: At least.

HUMAYUN: I mean, not that I'd want…

I wouldn't want a woman to have to see this.

BABUR: *(Realizing maybe for the first time.)* This was terrible. What we just did was terrible.

HUMAYUN: It was our job.

Babu, it was our job, okay?

(Beat.)

So is cleaning.
Let's clean.
Let's clean.

> *They just stand there for a moment. How does one even approach a mess like this?*
>
> *They drag the basket of hands into an alcove. As they do, BABUR sees the thousands of other baskets that have been dragged back there... he shudders when he sees them.*

BABUR: What do we do with all of those baskets of hands?

HUMAYUN: Burn them. Outside.

BABUR: That's going to smell terrible.

HUMAYUN: I know.

BABUR: We'll see them around. Probably begging. And they'll see us. They'll remember you and me, Huma. They hate us. Those guys hate us.

> *They start to mop, but realize they are just pushing around blood.*

HUMAYUN: Isn't there a drain?

BABUR: It's clogged.

HUMAYUN: Can we unclog it?

> *BABUR puts his hand through a deep pool, searching for the drain. He finds something and lifts a vile, disgusting lump of hair, flesh and fingers that have bound together in an unholy mess.*
>
> *BABUR makes a verbal sound of disgust as he holds it out and then discards it.*

HUMAYUN and BABUR both begin to clean the entire room thoroughly...a task that will take them until the end of the scene.

But initially, HUMAYUN, disgusted with the blood, has to take a moment.

HUMAYUN: Your flying invention with the seat-belt was a good idea. I too, have an idea.

(Beat.)

I have an invention, too. *A transportable hole.*

Proud of this, HUMAYUN looks to see if he got a reaction; he didn't.

HUMAYUN: It's literally a hole you could take anywhere with you. And you could attach it to anything. And anything you attached it to would suddenly have a hole in it. Say you wanted to go through a wall? You could. Or say you are trapped in a dungeon. Or you are in the desert and it is so hot! Hole in the ground, now you can sleep in some shade. Also there would be things to eat in the hole.

BABUR: What would there be to eat?

HUMAYUN: I don't know. Beef curry. Parathas.

BABUR: It wouldn't fall out?

HUMAYUN: What?

BABUR: Food. Wouldn't fall out? Of the hole?

HUMAYUN: No, it would be *in* the hole.

BABUR: But the hole's a hole.

HUMAYUN: A *transportable* hole.

BABUR: How would you carry it?

HUMAYUN: Carry what?

BABUR: The transportable hole.

HUMAYUN: It would have a sack.

BABUR: A sack?

HUMAYUN: Inside the sack: transportable hole.

BABUR: What if I were in the sack.

HUMAYUN: Why would you be in the sack?

BABUR: For example if I was.

HUMAYUN: It's not a very big sack. You wouldn't fit.

BABUR: It's a small sack?

HUMAYUN: Big enough only for the transportable hole.

BABUR: It's a small hole?

HUMAYUN: Small enough to fit in the sack, but then, as holes are, it could grow and shrink in size.

BABUR: But what if I were in the sack?

HUMAYUN: You wouldn't fit inside the sack, as I've said, it's a small sack.

BABUR: But say I was very small.

HUMAYUN: Suddenly you are very small.

BABUR: Yes.

HUMAYUN: Small enough to fit inside the sack.

BABUR: Yes. I'm trapped, see, inside the sack.

HUMAYUN: How did you shrink?

BABUR: There was a potion, from some witch.

HUMAYUN: Okay.

BABUR: So now I'm very small, and someone has gone and put me in the sack.

HUMAYUN: With the transportable hole?

BABUR: No, the transportable hole isn't there yet. It's out of the sack.

HUMAYUN: You took it out of the sack?

BABUR: I didn't take it, it was already out when I was captured and put in the sack.

HUMAYUN: Who took it out?

BABUR: The boss man who owns it.

HUMAYUN: Maybe the emperor.

BABUR: You would think the emperor.

HUMAYUN: Seeing as the transportable hole is probably a very rare, expensive thing.

BABUR: That's what I was thinking. Not everyone gets a transportable hole. Too many transportable holes would be a bad idea as they might take up everything, the whole world, and then what? What if everything was a hole? I have another invention, too, about something you could put inside clouds.

HUMAYUN: Wait, go back to when you are inside the sack.

BABUR: Oh yeah, because I've shrunken to a very small size.

HUMAYUN: How small, like a child?

BABUR: No, like a doll a child plays with.

HUMAYUN: That's very small. And you're in the sack.

BABUR: Trapped inside, because the boss man, probably the emperor, captured me and put me in there.

HUMAYUN: Punished for being too small.

BABUR: But because the sack I'm trapped in is also the sack with which to transport the transportable hole, the transportable hole is now put into the sack. With me. Now: I'm in a sack that has a hole in it. So: Can I escape?

HUMAYUN: Well, you could just go right through the hole.

BABUR: Exactly!

HUMAYUN: That's what the hole is for.

BABUR: But could the transportable hole... wouldn't it also fall through its own hole?

HUMAYUN: Could the hole fall through itself?

BABUR: It's a good question.

HUMAYUN: Sure, it could.

BABUR: Well if it could, then the sack isn't a very good sack with which to carry it.

HUMAYUN: That is true.

BABUR: Nothing could carry it.

HUMAYUN: Nothing could ever carry it.

BABUR: And then how do you take the hole places?

HUMAYUN: *(Disappointed in himself.)* You couldn't. Nobody could. It's a useless invention.

> Beat. HUMAYUN is angry at himself. BABUR looks to cheer him up.

BABUR: *(New idea.)* Unless you had two sacks! And the hole simply led to the other sack, so even if the hole went through itself, it would end up in the other sack, and then back again in the corresponding sack. Like an hourglass.

> *They smile at each other. Problem solved. They clean for awhile.*

BABUR: I have a lot of new ideas for inventions.
When I was...
When I...
When I was...

> *(He takes a deep breath, calming himself.)*

When I was chopping...?
I thought about things I would invent.
I thought there would be a thing, like tea maybe, that you could put in the clouds, and then, when it began to rain, the rain would be different colors, maybe, and also taste

sweet, and imagine if we were out in the rain and there were colors over everything, bright blues and greens and pinks and it also tasted really good… maybe it was also alcoholic, and so was like wine, and so you also got drunk. Cloud tea.

HUMAYUN: That's a fantastic invention.

BABUR: I have another invention which is an invisible house that is for a garden and you could plant things inside the house.
I also thought, my aeroplat, that would fly to the stars? You could make a smaller one that would just take you to Turkey.

HUMAYUN: Why would it take you to Turkey?

BABUR: It would fly you there.

HUMAYUN: But why Turkey necessarily? Why not somewhere else?

BABUR: This aeroplat would go to Turkey.
Ustad Isa was in Turkey once.

> *(Awkward beat.)*

He said there were compassionate whores in Turkey, and the air was cool.
So this particular aeroplat is going to Turkey.

HUMAYUN: Compassionate whores?

BABUR: Yeah.

> *Beat.*

HUMAYUN: How long does it take to get to Turkey?

BABUR: *(Beat; BABUR stops working… he stares into space.)* He was the only one who didn't scream.
Ustad Isa.
He didn't scream. He only looked at me and…

He was the smartest man in the kingdom, Huma. The smartest man on earth. He could do anything. And now... no hands.

Another awkward beat.

HUMAYUN: Everything is over now, okay?

BABUR: Everything is over?

HUMAYUN: Yeah.

BABUR: Imagine if you didn't have your hands.

HUMAYUN: No.

BABUR: No what?

HUMAYUN: No, I'm not going to imagine that.

BABUR: You should.

HUMAYUN: Why.

BABUR: After what we just did.

HUMAYUN: We just did our job.

BABUR: But just imagine what that must be like to have both your hands *chopped off* and then the stumps cauterized, and then sent back into the world to do... to do what?
To do what with the rest of your life?
How do you eat?
How do you drink?
How do you scratch an itch?
How do you wipe your ass, Huma?

HUMAYUN: I don't care, just shut up, okay?

BABUR: A man with no hands is a man who cannot be useful.
An unuseful man is a devil.

HUMAYUN: Tell me some other inventions.
Do you have other inventions?

Beat. Maybe HUMAYUN has succeeded in distracting BABUR from his slowly growing despair.

BABUR: What if the transportable hole had no bottom? Like I put it on the ground and I fall through it, and so I fall through the world, and I pop out on the other side, in some strange, far off land, as far away as you could possibly get from where we are… could the transportable hole do that?

> *Beat; they think.*

HUMAYUN: Maybe.

BABUR: I want the hole more than the aeroplat.

HUMAYUN: More than Turkey?

BABUR: More than Turkey.

HUMAYUN: More than compassionate whores?

BABUR: More than anything.

HUMAYUN: That they are *compassionate*… This is what sets them apart? Why did Ustad Isa use this particular word. Did he fall ill? They tended to him? Were they very good listeners?

> *(Beat.)*

Compassionate!

> *They clean.*

> *HUMAYUN, with a rag, scrubs the wooden chopping block. He has to really get in there and scrub. In doing so, his hands are placed directly on the chopping block.*

> *BABUR sees this as he passes by HUMAYUN, and stops in his tracks. HUMAYUN doesn't notice BABUR has stopped and is looking at him. HUMAYUN is concentrating intently on the chopping block, trying to scrub out the blood.*

> *BABUR is nearly in a trance, staring at HUMAYUN's hands.*

HUMAYUN: What?

> *BABUR snaps out of it, walks away.*

BABUR: Nothing.

HUMAYUN watches BABUR for a moment, slightly troubled by his friend's behavior. Then goes back to scrubbing the chopping block. He looks at the block.

HUMAYUN: It is true, though, what you say...

It's got to be a terrible thing. Spend sixteen years building Tajmahal... and then to not be able to build anything again. Chop off these hands... *So that nothing so beautiful as Tajmahal shall ever be built again.*

The Emperor is a serious man, bhai.

Nothing so beautiful ever built again.

(Beat; he cleans.)

You know when you think about it... I guess that means that the most beautiful thing ever made... will always be here, right in front of us, in our city.

So that at least is good...

We don't really have to worry about something more beautiful being built anywhere else.

We get the most beautiful thing, right here in Agra.

This fact suddenly has a deep effect on BABUR.

BABUR: Huma...

HUMAYUN: Yeah?

BABUR: *(Beginning to realize something.)* Do you understand what that means?

HUMAYUN: What *what* means?

BABUR: *(Growing realization.)* It means there will *never be anything as beautiful built ever again.*

(New revelation.)

And if nothing so beautiful is ever built again, that means that Beauty itself is dying. Right now, already, it's dying. It means that one day, it will be gone altogether.

(New realization.)

And it's my fault!

HUMAYUN: Come on, bhai…

BABUR: 400 years, 500 years from now, Huma, maybe sooner, there won't be anysuch thing as Beauty. It was executed, and the executioner was me.

I killed Beauty.

I killed Beauty…

(With rising recognition & horror of this.)

I killed Beauty!

HUMAYUN: No, you didn't, you didn't kill Beauty!

You didn't kill anything or anybody, you just did your job.

BABUR: Whether it was my job or not is besides the point!

HUMAYUN: It is exactly the point! It is the only point!

BABUR: I killed Beauty!

HUMAYUN: No, you didn't, okay? Nobody killed Beauty, you can't kill Beauty.

BABUR: You just said it yourself! You just said, nothing more beautiful would ever be built again… That we get the most beautiful thing ever made here in Agra… but the flip side to that is that if nothing else will ever be built that is as beautiful, it means that beauty has actually gone extinct, and so… And so… that's it. It's gone.

HUMAYUN: *(Thinking about it.)* I guess you're right.

Wow.

We killed Beauty.

BABUR: NO. You didn't kill Beauty, *I* killed beauty.

HUMAYUN: We did this thing together!

BABUR: I chopped! You cauterized!

HUMAYUN: That's semantics!

BABUR: I chopped, you cauterized, end of story. I did the damage. I removed the hands. I killed Beauty.

HUMAYUN: You know what, you don't ever give me credit for anything.

BABUR: I don't ever!? Since when?

HUMAYUN: Take your pick! My jokes aren't funny, only your jokes are funny. I'm not good at cards, only you're good at cards. My inventions are stupid, your inventions are interesting!

BABUR: I like the transportable hole!

HUMAYUN: It doesn't work! You can't transport it! And now I didn't kill Beauty, only you killed Beauty, even though I went fucking blind burning those bleeding stumps all night! I think I should at least be an accessory to the crime, okay mister? Jeez. It's like I didn't go through this whole ordeal with you tonight.

BABUR: It doesn't feel like you did.

HUMAYUN: And why is that?

BABUR: You don't care.

HUMAYUN: I don't care about what?

BABUR: You don't care that 20,000 men don't have their hands anymore.

HUMAYUN: How am I supposed to care about that? What is caring going to get me?

BABUR: It's just the truth, Huma.

HUMAYUN: If we hadn't done our jobs tonight, we'd be hanging by our necks in the royal courtyard getting our eyes pecked out by the royal crows. So excuse me if I don't wallow in some misbegotten guilt all night. Was it fucked up? Yes, it was. But I don't have to feel terrible about it.

BABUR: Yeah you do.

HUMAYUN: No I don't.

BABUR: This is why you don't get to say you killed Beauty, why only I killed Beauty, because you don't even care. You don't care about Beauty.

HUMAYUN: I do too care about Beauty.

BABUR: Fine, name one beautiful thing.

HUMAYUN: Tajmahal.

BABUR: Name another.

> *HUMAYUN starts to answer, but is stumped.*

BABUR: See you don't know any –

HUMAYUN: – Give me a second! Wine.

BABUR: Not beautiful just tasty.

HUMAYUN: Women.

BABUR: Doesn't count.

HUMAYUN: Women don't count.

BABUR: No.

HUMAYUN: *Women don't count as beautiful.*

BABUR: Different kind of beauty!

HUMAYUN: You're all over the place!

BABUR: I like Beauty. I have always liked Beauty. It matters to me. It has never mattered to you. You're only interested in Rules. And the King. And Your Father. And BEING A GOOD SOLDIER.

HUMAYUN: Birds!
Birds are beautiful.

> *They just stare at each other, not even knowing why they're fighting.*
>
> *HUMAYUN exits into the alcove, still working. As he does he shouts back these examples of beauty:*

HUMAYUN: *(O.S.)*
  Birds flocking: Beautiful.
  Hawks, Green parrots: Beautiful.
  Red Breasted jibjabs: Beautiful.
  Anything with feathers: Beautiful.
  See?
  Tell me *I* don't like beauty, I LOVE beauty, I'm a beauty
  EXPERT.

> *BABUR wipes his cheek. He sees there is blood on it, he wipes*
> *it again. And again. It grows as a tick. (Maybe he's been*
> *doing this for a while.) He suddenly can't stop wiping his face.*

> *HUMAYUN re-enters. He's cleaned himself up a bit.*

HUMAYUN: What's wrong, what are you doing?

BABUR: Got blood on my face.

HUMAYUN: You're *covered* in blood. We both are. Babur...

> *BABUR is nearly slapping himself, trying to remove one tiny*
> *stain, even though he's drenched in blood.*

BABUR: Won't come off! It won't come off!

HUMAYUN: Babur! BABUR, STOP! HEY!

> *HUMAYUN grabs BABUR in a bear hug to get him to stop.*
> *BABUR stops, shudders, slowly falls into HUMAYUN,*
> *suddenly overwhelmed with everything.*

BABUR: *(With deep grief.)* It's terrible what we did...

> *HUMAYUN gently brings BABUR to the floor, where they*
> *kneel together.*

HUMAYUN: Hey. Hey, look at me.

> *BABUR is traumatized. HUMAYUN touches his face, gently,*
> *almost as if BABUR were a child, waking from a nightmare.*

HUMAYUN: I'll wash your face, okay?

> *HUMAYUN goes to a clay urn and brings it beside BABUR,*
> *sitting, head in his hands.*

HUMAYUN: It's warm, the water is warm.

> *HUMAYUN pours the water slowly over BABUR's head. He does it again, smoothening out BABUR's hair, trying to comfort his friend. He pours another cup. It resembles a baptism.*
>
> *HUMAYUN takes BABUR's shirt off. He dries him off. He gets BABUR clean clothes and slowly, gently, like a parent with a child, helps BABUR clean and dress himself. HUMAYUN sings a tuneless song to BABUR as he does, softly, barely heard…*

HUMAYUN: *(Singing softly.)* Ohhhh Babu…

Babu Babu Babu…

Babu Babu Babu…

> *As BABUR becomes fully dressed…*

HUMAYUN: This morning, when we turned around to look…

When we saw Tajmahal…

I thought the moon had fallen.

I thought the moon had crashed in the river.

BABUR: It's prettier than the moon.

HUMAYUN: No. It's not.

SCENE 3

Lights up on the same guard post as the start of the play.

BABUR enters, ready to guard his post. He looks haggard.

There is the distant cacophony of the chopping, the screaming, the hissing and so forth. Everything gets louder.

HUMAYUN enters, and sees BABUR. He approaches him from behind, but BABUR doesn't notice, lost in a nightmare.

HUMAYUN calls out to him by name, but he cannot be heard over the sounds… He calls again… finally…

HUMAYUN: BABUR! BABUR! BABUR!

*The sounds cut out entirely. There is just the sound of night.
Maybe a cricket.*

*BABUR turns around and stands guard. HUMAYUN as well,
takes his post.*

HUMAYUN: You're here. You're on time.

(Beat.)

BABUR: I had a terrible dream.

HUMAYUN: *(Barely able to conceal.)* I have some good news!

BABUR: Worst nightmare of my life, bhai.

HUMAYUN: Do you want to tell me the dream first, or can I
tell you the good news that I have?

BABUR: It was about aeroplats.

HUMAYUN: Okay, so your dream…

BABUR: They were so loud, they made a terrible sound.
And there were hundreds of them. They were weapons,
the aeroplats themselves were actually weapons, flying
weapons, and… I mean, think about it, Huma… with
aeroplats, you could defeat any army of men on elephants
without a problem.

But, these were the aeroplats of a distant army. And they
were coming for us.

HUMAYUN: For us?

BABUR: For Hindustan. And do you know how they would
know when they found us? Guess.

HUMAYUN: I don't know.

BABUR: Guess.

HUMAYUN: I don't know, I don't know how aeroplats work!

BABUR: Tajmahal. They'll see it, shining like the moon, and
the first thing they'll destroy is that. And so the emperor
stood above us. And he told us that there was a large piece
of cloth. The biggest in the world. It was black… it was

44

just like the transportable hole, Huma, and he told us, if
we could all grab a piece of this fabric, and run with it, it
would billow and lift, and we could drape it just so over
Tajmahal, and hide Tajmahal. Hide it from the aeroplats.

And so we ran to the cloth, and we all tried to grab it, but
we couldn't, we couldn't, Huma, because none of us had
any hands.

> *(Beat.)*

Even I didn't. Neither did the emperor. Everyone had
lost their hands. And so we couldn't grip the giant cloth,
and then the aeroplats came and they destroyed Tajmahal
instantly, and the rest of Hindustan began to burn.

> *Awkward beat.*

HUMAYUN: So do you want to hear my good news?

BABUR: Sure.

HUMAYUN: You're gonna like this.

BABUR: Okay.

HUMAYUN: I'm still in shock about it.

BABUR: Yeah?

HUMAYUN: Where do I begin?

BABUR: I don't know.

HUMAYUN: So…

BABUR: Yeah?

HUMAYUN: I was speaking with my father.

BABUR: Yeah??

HUMAYUN: Because we carried out our duties last night with
such… efficiency… And also because we cleaned up
so well – they were really impressed with how well we
cleaned up – my father has told me that you and I… are
assigned to the Imperial Harem.

(Beat.)

We're on Harem duty.

BABUR: Harem Duty?

HUMAYUN: Harem Duty.

BABUR: We get to go into the Imperial Harem?!

HUMAYUN: See? This is how it goes… People notice. Elders notice. We did our job last night and we cleaned up so well – they were really impressed with the clean up job – and now we get to accompany the Emperor himself to the Harem. And Guard him. In the *HAREM*.

BABUR: That's amazing!

HUMAYUN: Weren't you just saying you wanted to see the inside of the Harem before you die?

BABUR: I was.

HUMAYUN: And here we go!

BABUR: Your father is the best.

HUMAYUN: It wasn't because of my father! It was because we carried out our duties so well!

BABUR: Sure yeah. I mean, that too.
When?

HUMAYUN: Tomorrow.

BABUR: Tomorrow?!

HUMAYUN: No more Dawn Watch.

BABUR: Tomorrow!

HUMAYUN: Big blammo promotion, bhai.

BABUR: We're on Harem Duty.

HUMAYUN: No: We are *Personal Guards to the Emperor in the Imperial Harem.*
I love saying that.

BABUR: What do we do? How do we do it? Why do we do it? How does one *do* Harem Duty?

HUMAYUN: We accompany the Emperor from the palace to the Imperial Harem. And then we follow him wherever he goes in the Harem. And we stand at either side of him when he sits at the royal desk.

BABUR: Naked women!

HUMYAUN: If there are naked women – which I highly doubt – we can't look or touch or even acknowledge them unless it is in service of the emperor himself.

BABUR: Or what?

HUMAYUN: Or what what?

BABUR: Say I meet a nice girl in there and we –

HUMAYUN: You get executed. So don't do that.

BABUR: The Imperial Harem!

HUMAYUN: You understand, this is unprecedented.

BABUR: Yeah!

HUMAYUN: It's a reward. Everyone knew last night was a shit job. And we did it and we did it well and we did not complain, so... Harem Duty.

> *(Beat.)*

You understand that, right?

BABUR: Yeah, sure, I do.

HUMAYUN: We do not always get pleasant tasks.

BABUR: Of course not.

HUMAYUN: But we work our way to the better tasks, the more pleasant tasks.

BABUR: Of course.

HUMAYUN: You understand how this works, right?

BABUR: Yes! I understand! Why do you keep asking me that?

HUMAYUN: Because sometimes I think you don't understand.

BABUR: I get it! We do shit jobs first, and then we get better jobs, so long as we do the shit jobs well and without complaint.

HUMAYUN: Exactly.

BABUR: Not complicated.

HUMAYUN: Exactly.

> *(Awkward beat.)*

You just seemed... last night...

BABUR: I seemed what?

HUMAYUN: You seemed...

BABUR: Like what?

HUMAYUN: You seemed like you didn't understand that.

> *Beat.*

BABUR: I had a rough night.

HUMAYUN: Okay, well, *you're not allowed to have a rough night, Mister.*

BABUR: I'm embarrassed, okay?

> *(Beat.)*

I'm embarrassed by how I acted last night, Huma, I'm sorry.
I didn't mean to...
I couldn't stop...

> *(Beat; he gets angry.)*

You got to cauterize them!

HUMAYUN: This again? Chopping was not worse than cauterizing!

BABUR: It was different...

HUMAYUN: Let's not fight about this.

BABUR: The point is…

The point is…

There is no point.

I'm sorry.

I should have been stronger.

> *Long beat.*

HUMAYUN: *(Changes his tact; is kind.)* You were strong.

You are strong.

You're here, this morning, at your post, on time for the first time in your life. After nightmares, and after last night.

You're strong, Babur.

The point is, you need to stop thinking about it and you need to stop talking about it.

BABUR: Stop thinking. Stop talking.

HUMAYUN: You're lucky we're old friends, old pals. Some other bastard would've already pegged you for a traitor or a bitch, and then what? Words spread out across the guard and pop! You have a traitorous bitch of a reputation, and that's not good. Reputations stain deeper than blood.

BABUR: You didn't tell anyone…?

HUMAYUN: Of course I didn't.

You're my bhai.

> *(Beat.)*

But stop thinking about it and stop talking about it and let's just enjoy our good fortune here, Babu… Imperial Harem. You and me. Standing guard, right next to the emperor.

BABUR: Right next to him?

HUMAYUN: Maybe a little behind, just a shred. So we don't impede his vision, etcetera.

BABUR: Just a little behind.

HUMAYUN: The emperor himself, Most Supreme Glorious Ruler of Hindustan, Shah Jahan, son of Jahangir, son of Akbar, son of Humayun –

BABUR: – Your namesake...

HUMAYUN: My namesake... son of Babur. Your namesake.

BABUR: My namesake.

HUMAYUN: Babur, first Mughal Emperor of Hindustan. The Royal Line! And who's there to the left and the right?

BABUR: You and me.

HUMAYUN: Me and you. Standing proud, regal as the Man himself. Protecting him. Daring some piss-shit fellow to come at him with ill intentions.

> *(Imitating sounds of efficient violence.)*

> *Swach! Swaah! Scccck!*

> Done. Bingho-bangho, sent to the grave. Quick-stuffed.

BABUR: *Yeah!*

HUMAYUN: Yeah. It takes years to make these strides. Years. But a job like last night's doesn't come along that often. We have an honest battle story, bhai. From now until we're old and grey, we'll be telling our sons and grandsons about the night of the Forty Thousand Hands.

BABUR: I thought we were supposed to stop thinking, stop talking...

HUMAYUN: Stop thinking, stop talking *like you are.*

BABUR: Like me...

HUMAYUN: Yeah, like how you are thinking and talking with this air of regret.

BABUR: *Regret.*

HUMAYUN: Yeah. *Regret.* I'm saying, *brag about it.*

BABUR: *(Sad, but trying to put on a good face.)* You're right.

HUMAYUN: Right?

BABUR: Absolutely. Brag. *I cut off 40,000 hands! Ho!*

HUMAYUN: Imperial Harem, bhai.

BABUR: Standing right next to the emperor.

HUMAYUN: Or a shred behind him so as to not impede his view.

BABUR: Standing a shred behind him. Guarding him.
   Guarding Shah Jahan.

HUMAYUN: Proud as cocks.

BABUR: I won't be late.

HUMAYUN: You better not be late.

BABUR: Women everywhere in the Harem.

HUMAYUN: And eunuchs.

BABUR: Those poor bastards.

HUMAYUN: And the King.

BABUR: And Us. Standing just a little bit behind him.

> *(Starts to realize something.)*

   Just a shred behind… the emperor.
   Right behind him.
   Him, sitting right there. At the Royal Desk.
   Me, just a little behind…
   A shred behind him.
   A shred behind him…

HUMAYUN: Yeah. Why are you saying it like that?

BABUR: *(Realizing at this moment.)* Humayun!

HUMAYUN: What?

BABUR: I have an idea.

HUMAYUN: Okay.

BABUR: Hear me out.

HUMAYUN: Okay.

BABUR: You probably won't like it at first.

HUMAYUN: Just tell me.

BABUR: But if you just give it a second.

HUMAYUN: An invention?

BABUR: No. Yes. Maybe. A little bit of that.
So…
We're at the Imperial Harem. Tomorrow.

HUMAYUN: Yeah.

BABUR: And we're standing just a shred behind the Emperor at the Royal Desk.

HUMAYUN: Just a shred behind him.

BABUR: And so… at one point, when maybe nobody else is in the room… we'll make a secret signal to each other.

HUMAYUN: What kind of secret signal?

BABUR: Something really subtle.

HUMAYUN: We can't move, though.

BABUR: We'll figure something out.

HUMAYUN: Why are we making the secret signal?

BABUR: I'm getting to that…

HUMAYUN: Okay.

BABUR: When we do, make the secret signal, you grab the emperor's head, pull it back, and then I'll slice his neck wide fucking open.

HUMAYUN: Wait… say again?

BABUR: Let's kill the King.

HUMAYUN: Whoa… WHAT!? What the hell are you talking about?
What did you just say!?

BABUR: You said you were gonna hear me out.

HUMAYUN: You can't say that, and you can't mean that, and and and… LOOK: I'm going to let you shut your treasonous face and take up your position and we'll never speak of it again.

BABUR: I didn't realize it until just now, but this is the only thing to do.

HUMAYUN: Please… Don't go crazy. Don't go crazy on me, Babur…

BABUR: Not crazy. Listen. First of all, I killed Beauty.

HUMAYUN: *You didn't kill beauty!*

BABUR: Okay, *we* killed Beauty. *We* did, okay?

HUMAYUN: No, shut up, okay! It is fine to have a philosophical conversation about aesthetics, but you just threatened to *kill the King!*

BABUR: Yeah, I'm gonna do that. We should do it together.

HUMAYUN: Babur, please, stop! They can kill you just for saying that! You're out of your mind!

BABUR: Nope. Thinking clearly here, bhai. Have a good sense of things here, bhai…

HUMAYUN: Oh, very clearly. We chop off the emperor's head tomorrow morning… Then what!

BABUR: Well, that's the rest of the plan. We exit the office, calmly, walking through the halls of the Harem. Nobody will speak to us. We leave the Harem, we go to the Royal stables, we take two horses, and then we ride out to the jungle.

HUMAYUN: That's your plan!?

BABUR: Remember our sandalwood raft in the trees? We stayed three nights in the jungle! This time, we'll make a better one, a bigger one, with a roof, and near some water, and we can hunt animals and eat them, and we could live just you and me, Huma, out in the wild… away from everything, away from the world. Away from the King and your father and the rules, and far away from the memory of what we did. Nobody will ever make us do anything again.

Wouldn't that be good?

HUMAYUN: Why can't we do that without killing the King?

BABUR: I mean, we could… but killing the King… that's like the main part.

We kill him, so Beauty can live.

HUMAYUN: You're crazy.

BABUR: Tell me you wouldn't want to live out in the jungle away from the world!

HUMAYUN: I wouldn't! Okay? That sounds awful! I don't want to have to hunt for my food, I don't want to sleep outside every night and I certainly don't want to risk my neck murdering the emperor!

Babur! Wake up! Because I don't think you actually understand *anything*:

There is the King. And He is at the Center.

And there are those who serve him, closely, like us, and so we are *near* the Center, and so our lives are good and we eat well.

And then there's the rest of the world out there, balancing on the edge of things.

And they do not eat well.

But yesterday… and today…

If people see Tajmahal and suddenly think that this wonderful, unbelievable thing was created by 20,000 ordinary men, then they begin to wonder about changing their lives.

And if enough people do that, then the edge might come for the center. And the center could be cast away.

And then we're fucked.

So that's why we did this.

Your sword, my cauterizing iron, those baskets of hands…

This is called Keeping the Peace.
We have a good life, Babu. And I appreciate it. I like the world.

BABUR: You like the world.

HUMAYUN: Yeah.

BABUR: *This* world, you're saying. You like *this* world… where we have to behand 20,000 men in one night. Where we have to kill off Beauty like a wounded animal. Where anything we might ever feel or think or say could cause us to be executed simply because the Emperor is shithouse crazy?

HUMAYUN: There is either allegiance to the Emperor, or there is death. I'm choosing Not Death. So should you. I'm sorry you can't handle the sight of a couple gallons of blood, but grow some balls, yaar. Seriously.

BABUR: If you don't want to help me tomorrow, that's fine, but I am going to kill the King.

HUMAYUN: You think you can kill the King? I'll be right on his other side, bhai. And as my oaths dictate, any man who raises a hand to His Most Glorious Emperor Shah Jahan will pay for it with his *life*.
You want me to kill you tomorrow morning? Is that what you want?

BABUR: I don't want Tajmahal to be the last beautiful thing ever made.

HUMAYUN: If the King decrees that Beauty is dead, then Beauty is dead.

BABUR: *(In HUMA's face.)* Then fuck the King. Beauty shall live.

> *BABUR walks away from HUMAYUN, repeating this, getting louder, as if to proclaim this to the kingdom.*

BABUR: Fuck the King! Beauty shall live!
FUCK THE KING! BEAUTY SHALL LIVE!

> *(At top of his lungs.)*

FUCK THE KING! BEAUTY SHALL LIVE!

HUMAYUN jumps on BABUR to stop him, quiet him, and throws him to the ground, stunning BABUR.

HUMAYUN: You are under arrest for… for… you are arrested for BLASPHEMY! BLASPHEMY!

BABUR: What are you talking about?

HUMAYUN: *(Quietly to BABUR.)* Listen, bhai… it's just "blasphemy". Three days in jail. That's it. You go to jail, you cool your head, you stop this crazy talk.

BABUR: Get OFF, stop, Huma!

HUMAYUN: If they hear what you're saying they will have an elephant *trample you to death!* It's treason, bhai!

BABUR: Let me go… Damnit, Humayun!

HUMAYUN: *(Quietly.)* You'll do three days and then you'll come out and it'll be just me and you.
You and me. No more talk of beauty. No more talk of killing the king.
Okay? Okay. Okay. Guards! Guards! GUARDS!

SCENE 4

A prison cell. BABUR is chained to the wall.

BABUR: This is BULLSHIT.

HUMAYUN enters. He looks changed… he may have just been crying.

BABUR: There he is. Traitorous bastard. You throw your own bhai into jail?! Is that what you do?! Remind me to never tell you anything ever again.

(Beat.)

I should have never opened my mouth around you, O son of the Big Boss on High.

(Beat; BABUR takes a new approach.)

You really thought I would have gone along with it? You thought me, Babur, was going to kill the emperor?!

(Beat.)

I just needed to talk through it, was all, Huma. God, you overreact.

HUMAYUN: *I* overreact!?

(Beat; quietly.)

They would have put you to death for what you said!

BABUR: So now I'm in jail. Charged with blasphemy. Is that what happened?

HUMAYUN: You wouldn't shut up!

BABUR: When have I ever shut up? What day since we were boys did I not blabber to you about this or that, about fancies and prophecies and inventions or what dreams I had…

(Beat.)

But now, today, out of the blue, you arrest me?

HUMAYUN: You never before plotted to murder the King.

BABUR: I wouldn't have done it. I couldn't. I don't know if I can stand the sight of blood anymore.

HUMAYUN: Some guard you would make, then.

HUMAYUN starts to cry.

BABUR: Are you goddamn *crying?*

Okay okay, I forgive you already, my good God, *this* I have never seen! Humayun crying like a little girl! Trust me on one point, mister, you will *never hear the end of this.* Never. Not from me. I will never let you forget that one night you cried your face off out of guilt for your poor sweet Babur.

HUMAYUN now groans a terrible groan – haunted, awful.

An awkward beat follows it; something is up.

BABUR: I can swallow three days in here. This is a *palace*. I was
raised in worse.

(Beat.)

What are you even *doing* here? You missed me so much
you couldn't let me languish in solitary fashion?
Is that it, boss?
Did you miss me?

HUMAYUN: You're weak.

BABUR: I'm weak?

HUMAYUN: Since when do you love people *so much* you can't
bear to hurt them?

BABUR: I could never bear to hurt anyone.
You know this.
I apologize to a chicken before I snap his neck.
I'm weak.
I like being weak.

HUMAYUN: That doesn't make any sense.

BABUR: Who knows?

HUMAYUN: Nobody wants to be weak. Nobody prefers to be
weak.

BABUR: I appreciate what you did.

HUMAYUN: What?

BABUR: Arresting me. You probably saved my life.
You were right. I was all worked up.
I'm calm now. I'll be good.

HUMAYUN gets up and slowly.

HUMAYUN: *(Quietly.)* I'm sorry, bhai.

*HUMAYUN walks away from a bewildered BABUR and,
walking to an alcove, pulls out the wood chopping block.*

BABUR: Humayun… what are you doing? What are you… why is THAT THERE!?

HUMAYUN: I'm sorry, bhai…

> *HUMAYUN detaches BABUR's chains and suddenly and forcefully pulls BABUR across the room to the chopping block, where he is able to chain BABUR's arms and hands down, across the block.*

BABUR: No, no no no! Huma, what are you doing?! What are you…STOP! STOP HUMAYUN STOP!

> *HUMAYUN backs away from BABUR and the block and has to sit in against the wall again, holding his head in his hands.*

BABUR: Huma, what's going on… you said Blasphemy! You said three days in jail! What the fuck is this?! You're not taking my hands, Huma! Come on!

HUMAYUN: I have to.

BABUR: NO! WHY!? NO!

HUMAYUN: Babu…

BABUR: What are you TALKING ABOUT?

HUMAYUN: Just QUIET, or it could get worse… Okay? Just QUIET PLEASE…

BABUR: You can't take my hands. Huma, it's me, it's Babur, okay? You can't chop off your bhai's hands!

HUMAYUN: I thought blasphemy would be the best… charge… three days in jail.

BABUR: Yeah! That's what you said!

HUMAYUN: I had to invent some story, so I did and I told the mansabdar my tall tale, and he believed it just fine… but then I had to go before my father…
And he knew I was lying.
He looks through me. He can read my mind…
And so I told him…
Everything about you, about what you said, and then I…

Babu…

I threw myself at his feet and begged him to not kill you.

I cried and I begged…

He was disgusted in me.

But he said you could live. But only if…

Only if I take your hands.

BABUR: No! No! No!

> *HUMAYUN starts weeping. BABUR just stares at him.*

HUMAYUN: I have to do it.

> *HUMAYUN goes and retrieves a large sword.*

BABUR: *(Trying a gentler approach.)* Listen, Huma, you don't have to.

There's nothing you have to do. You're smart, you can figure something out.

> *(Beat; he waits.)*

Just let me go. Say I escaped. I'll run off. Nobody will ever hear from me again… *Just don't take my hands…*

HUMAYUN: If I don't they'll kill you.

BABUR: No, they won't. They won't! I'll escape! On my own… you don't even have to help me, just let me out of these chains and… Humayun… Huma… come on…

> *HUMAYUN readies himself to do it.*

BABUR: NO! No, don't you do this, Humayun, don't you… you can't do this. NO! Listen to me, I know you, Huma, this will *fuck you up*…

This is what we're going to do. I'll scream so everyone will think you did what you needed to do, and then I'll –

> *HUMAYUN brings his sword down on BABUR's wrists;*
>
> *BABUR tries to scream, but no sound comes out.*

The hands don't come off with one stroke. He brings down his sword again. Still not good enough. A third time, and blood sprays all over HUMAYUN's face.

BABUR lies on the ground, handless, screaming. HUMAYUN stares at him in shock for a moment, but then turns, grabs a cauterizing iron out of an oven, and walks to BABUR and cauterizes his stumps. Then, with cloth, wraps them.

He walks back to the oven and throws the iron into it. He stands still, facing the wall for a long time, while BABUR writhes on the floor, no longer screaming, silently gasping.

HUMAYUN exits.

BABUR: Huma…?

Huma…

(Quietly.)

Don't go.

SCENE 5

Night. HUMAYUN stands guard outside the Taj, the same spot. It is ten years later.

HUMAYUN: Who's There! Show yourself! There is a Royal Curfew presently imposed!

Nobody is there, but HUMAYUN is convinced someone is hiding in the shadows…

HUMAYUN: In the name of his most supreme Emperor Aurangzeb Alamgir, show your face!

There really is nobody there.

HUMAYUN lowers his sword. He almost has to look back – he could have sworn someone was there. He was almost hoping someone was.

HUMAYUN: *(Quietly, hopeful, almost as if he were still a boy.)* Hello?

He takes a moment, but then goes back to his guard stance.

He stands alone for a long moment.

The same bird call from the start of the play.

HUMAYUN looks up at it, recognizing it, hearing it is salt in his terrible wound. The bird sings again

It's almost as if HUMAYUN is hearing the voice of BABUR. He remembers his friend, he remembers everything.

Another bird calls. And another. A cacophony of birds fills the world. HUMAYUN is suddenly afraid…

The deep rumble of a jungle… insects, wind, trees, the cry of an animal… and lightning bugs are everywhere.

An ivy begins to grow everywhere around HUMAYUN, and trees grow out of the air, and surround him, as he finds himself between two worlds: the Taj in Agra, and a jungle.

HUMAYUN: Babur…! Babur…!

What are those sounds…

They're everywhere…

In the branches above him, there is nestled a wooden platform. From the branches of the trees, onto the platform, climbs BABUR, several years younger, shirtless, bathed in sweat, standing proudly on his sandalwood raft in the trees. He's buoyant.

BABUR: Creatures! Of the jungle!

HUMAYUN: Yeah, but *what creatures…!*

BABUR: Always worrying! Humayun the fretful!

HUMAYUN: We are LOST IN THE JUNGLE!

BABUR: We're not "lost"! We just got separated from our troop.

HUMAYUN: That's *lost!*

A distant roar…

HUMAYUN: What the hell is that?

BABUR: Probably a tiger.

HUMAYUN: *A tiger!?*

BABUR: That's why we have this, that's why we crafted this perfect little platform, our little sandalwood raft in the trees! I'd like to see some tiger climb up here and poke his nose.

HUMAYUN: Tigers can climb trees!

BABUR: I say let them! They'll take one look at this…

> *BABUR does a dance on the platform…*

HUMAYUN: There's other things that can get up here. Snakes. Insects. Snakes.

BABUR: Huma! This is fun! We got separated from our troop!

HUMAYUN: Yeah, and I would like to find them!

BABUR: And I would very much prefer to NOT find them. Those fellows are right cocksucking banditfuckers.

HUMAYUN: We're really going to spend the night on this *thing?* In a *tree?* In the *jungle?*

BABUR: It's sandalwood. It has this smell… Mosquitos won't come near… and neither will snakes… The smell is distinct.

HUMAYUN: *(Sniffs the air.)* I do love that smell.

> *(Beat.)*

Look at this platform! It is pretty good. We *made* this. We *made* this with our *swords.*

BABUR: It's probably the greatest thing I've ever made.

HUMAYUN: Really?

BABUR: Yeah.

HUMAYUN: I don't know about that. I once carved a piece of wood to look like a bird. It looked just like a bird. That was probably the best thing I've ever made. This is second.

BABUR: You carve wood into birds?

HUMAYUN: I used to. Not so much anymore. My Dad thinks it's wasteful of my time. I dunno.

A loud shriek. BABUR gets a little scared.

BABUR: *What was that?!*

HUMAYUN: *(Smiles.)* That was a bat.

They laugh a little together.

BABUR: Wouldn't you rather be lost forever? Wouldn't that be so much better than going back to the troop and the army and Agra and everything? Living out here? Away from everyone.

HUMAYUN: I don't want to be lost forever!

BABUR: It might be more interesting, is all I'm saying.

(Seeing something in the distance.)

Hey, Humayun... Look!

HUMAYUN doesn't see.

HUMAYUN: What?

BABUR: Through these branches... Look at that...! I can't believe I didn't see that...! What *is* that?!

HUMAYUN cranes his head, and then sees it.

HUMAYUN: Oh whoa... WOW.

BABUR: What is that, a lake?

HUMAYUN: Yeah, it's a... pink lake.

BABUR: No, there's gotta be something on it. What the hell is it?

HUMAYUN: It's moving...

BABUR: Yeah, what is it... It's something on the water...

Beat; they crane their necks, trying to see...

HUMAYUN: It's birds!

BABUR: Birds?

HUMAYUN: Yeah, they're birds, sitting on the water...

BABUR: The entire thing is birds… that entire lake, every inch, is covered by a bird?

HUMAYUN: Yeah… a pink and purple bird.

BABUR: And green too? Or is that the water…?

HUMAYUN: Pink purple and green birds… look how beautiful, huh?

BABUR: There must be millions of them.

HUMAYUN: At least. What kind of bird is that… its… uhmmm… chiff-chaff? …Or maybe it's a…

> *Suddenly the immense sound of wings fills the space, both men are startled by it, and they both watch a gargantuan flock of birds lift off the lake and fly directly over them. It lasts a long time. They keep flying, right over them. It's a spiritual experience for both of them.*

> *Over the beating of wings… Both men looking straight up…*

BABUR: Huma…

HUMAYUN: Yeah…

BABUR: You see that…!?

HUMAYUN: Yeah! Yeah!

BABUR: You see that!?

HUMAYUN: Yeah! I see it! I see it!

> *They both laugh hysterically, and then almost cry.*

BABUR: Wow.

HUMAYUN: Wow.

BABUR: Wow.

HUMAYUN: Wow.

> *Then all the birds are gone. It's silent again.*

> *The jungle disappears, BABUR disappears, only HUMAYUN is left, back in Agra, guarding, alone.*

He takes a moment to hold on to his memory of BABUR and the raft in the trees and the past – the only place, for him, where beauty might live.

And then he goes back into a proper guarding position. He stands there, in silence, for a long time.

END OF PLAY

WWW.OBERONBOOKS.COM